MW00768590

Hill
Tauk

2

Publisher: Whispering Hope
P.O. Box 814, Mars Hill, NC 28754

Editor: Ben Brouke
Cover Photo Courtesy: Yellow Bird Company
Cover Design: Whispering Hope Publishing
Copyright (C), Ben Brouke 1998, All Rights Reserved

ISBN: 0-9658565-0-X

To order your personal autographed copy of this book, send $6.99 + $2.75
Shipping and Handling (USA) or $9.99 plus $3.75 Shipping and Handling
(CANADA) NC Residents add 6% Sales Tax.

TO: Whispering Hope Publishing
    P.O. Box 814
    Mars Hill, NC 28754

Printed in the United States of America

Contents

PREFACE

Everything is changing so fast that I wish we could go back to the days when a power lunch was a big bowl of Soup beans, a pone of cornbread, a big onion, and a tall glass of milk. To anyone that thinks this book is an insult, let me explain further.

As far as the Dictionary part of this book goes, I would guess it's about as close to the old English as you can get.
for example; there is a city in Connecticut that is spelled Greenwich, if you pronounced it the way it was spelled to a resident of that city, they are going to be upset with you. They pronounce it "GRINNICH," Ok, Now lets say you are sitting on your porch, and your neighbor is coming out of the driveway and she has the car in reverse, and you say she is coming out "BACKERDS."

Now, I would like some Yankee to explain to me why it's ok to pronounce Greenwich, "GRINNICH," but it is wrong to say "BACKERDS." Another thing is that people get Hillbillies Mixed up with Red Necks. Hillbillies only come from a few choice southern states and Rednecks come from all over, but to say one or the other is all good or all bad, would be like saying all Yankees are bad because of a few snobs.

In my wondering days I have known a lot of good Yankees as well as a lot of good southerners. Snobs also come from all over. But there is a difference. Yankee snobs think the earth is flat, Southern snobs know the earth is flat.

The word "AGITIZER" is used a few times in this book, but it is not in the dictionary, it should be, for it describes someone who is a fun type prankster who could also make you smile, laugh, giggle, cackle, snort and put you in an all around good mood.

In putting this book together we used that new fangled thing called a computer. Since I don't know a mouse from a virus, I needed a lot of help. I wish to thank two good friends, Joan Davis and Glen Bryant. Also a very big thanks to my very nice sister-in-law, K. Joyce Walker and to my darling wife who must have the patience of Job to put up with me all of these years.
And most of all, a very special thanks to my Lord and Savior **Jesus Christ.**

BEN BROUKE

INTRODUCTION

Just a few words to let you know what it was like growing up in Scott County, Virginia, in the 30's and 40's. We had a farm on a little over one hundred acres. We grew just about everything we ate plus tobacco. It seems like I was the one elected to take the corn to the mill to get ground for corn bread. We had a sack that was made for flour and meal. The meal would not come through the sack nor would anything get into the meal. I would take it on a mule with no saddle. On the way to the mill was the hardest because the corn would shift around and sometimes fall off and me with it. Coming back was easy because the corn meal would not shift and it made a soft saddle.

There is not much to say about my ancestors, except in 1843 after the death of my paternal great grandfather. My great grandmother was swindled out of 32,000 acres of land. I am told that my great Grandfather had put on the land records a document that stated "This land belongs to me and my heirs from now and forevermore, and never to be sold."

In the early part of the 1900's it was missing from the records.

My maternal grandfather was a Confederate soldier and saw Stonewall Jackson shot off his horse. When the war was over he was a doctor and a minister.

I am sure you have heard all the stories about how far someone walked to school, but I would like to tell you this. When my youngest son was seventeen years old we were going to go where I grew up. About two days before we left I heard him talking to a friend on the phone. He was telling him how his Dad walked three miles to school up hill both ways in knee deep snow. When we got there the first place we went was the school. From the school to our gate it was three miles and one tenth. With over a quarter mile to walk from the gate to the house. After we got back home a few days later he was talking to his

8

friend again. He told him that I did walk over three miles and it was up hill both ways. I remember the road that went by our place was two tracks. It ended at each end at a main gravel road. There was a stream that ran along in the road about three or four hundred feet at each end. I was fifteen years old before we got electricity, and the phone did not come until long after I left.

There are some stories about moonshining, but it was not a big operation. We just made a small amount to buy the necessities with. I can remember at least a half dozen times the revenue officers coming, but they never found a still in operation or any whiskey. My mother and sisters would have nothing to do with it. The funny part is the last two or three times my brother Henry put together the mash, it would not ferment. My sisters had put salt in it when nobody was looking. Henry finally said it was time to quit. All my brothers and sisters turned out to be good citizens; it just took me a lot longer and still working on it.

All the stories in this book are true except two, and maybe you should wonder about them. The names have been changed to protect the guilty as well as the innocent.

BEN BROUKE
1998

THE CONSPIRACY

You see these guys here? Their names are Billy Ed and
Eddy Bill. Well, we are going to get something straightened
out here and now. You see, there has been a wide spread
conspiracy to portray them as hillbillies, and they are not. It
all started in New York City, on a Friday in the middle of
May in 1928. Now here is this small but successful business
ran by four brothers.One's name is Rupert, and his wife's
name is Gretchen, and they have twin sons, 8 years old. Yes,
you guessed it, their names are Billy Ed and Eddy Bill.
Rupert was on his way home this Friday and his pockets were
picked for the fifth time in the last two months.When he got
home, his wife was in tears.

Billy Ed and Eddy Bill had been beaten up at school, and Gretchen was mugged coming home from shopping and all the groceries were taken.This family is very close. Nothing is more important to Rupert than the safety of his wife and kids. So they talked long into the night.

Finally, some decisions were made. Saturday, Rupert got with his brothers and told them he wanted all his money out of the business and sell his shares to them. They just about disowned him, but they agreed. Monday morning, Rupert was on his way to the southern mountains. Where exactly, we have not been able to pin down. It could have been in any one of six states. When he got off the train, Rupert bought land so far back in the mountains that moonlight is always two days late getting there. He also bought mules, tools, a sled, and a lot of other supplies plus one book on"How to build a log house with your own timber",and another on farming and how to live off the land. Somehow he managed to get everything to his property.

Then he started to work. He worked seven days a week from sun up to sun down. Towards the end of October, he was ready to go get his family. Of course since he was concerned about them when he left New York, he had made arrangements for someone to look after them so they would not have to go out of the house. When they got settled in their new house, they all agreed never to go out of the mountains for any reason.

Now ten years have passed, and the brothers in New York are a little concerned. Maybe they were a little too hard on Rupert. They discussed the situation a few days and decided that all three would go and visit him. So they loaded up the car with what they needed. They also took their camera and the directions Rupert had given them and left. When they got there, it was nothing like what they expected. Oh, Rupert and Gretchen looked fine, but Billy Ed and Eddy Bill were another story.

For twins, they looked nothing alike. Billy Ed was six foot four and weighed about 140 pounds. Eddy Bill was five foot seven and weighed 215 pounds. Both were wearing homespun clothes that were about to fall off them. The pant legs on both were torn about half off. They had on old slouch hats and they were both barefooted. It is a fact that no red-blooded hillbilly would be caught dead looking like this. The brothers stayed a few days. As they were about to leave, Rupert spotted the camera. He insisted pictures should be taken of the whole family.On the way home to New York, the brothers were discussing the film in the camera. The decision was to destroy it when they got home.

Because they wanted no one to see those pictures.

They Forgot.

A few days later, one of their wives found the film and took it in for developing. Then the kids got a hold of the pictures.

Now it's a few months later and everything is going fine. The three brothers are throwing a party at this big park. All their friends, neighbors, and business associates are invited. All together there are about two hundred people.Out come the pictures of Billy Ed and Eddy Bill.

The pictures are being passed around. Everyone there is wanting to know who those strange people are. The brothers have a problem. Now the conspiracy starts. The brothers go into a huddle and come up with a solution. Oh yes, in the southern mountains, everyone lives like this. You can see them all over the hills. Within the next year, half, the people at the party have gone looking for those strange people, and not finding them. They came looking for a trophy and most of them decide they will not go back without one. So they fake some pictures. Within five years, we have Yankees with cameras crawling all over the hills.

And most of them are going back with fake pictures. All over New York, in a lot of homes, hang those fake pictures with a caption, "Shot in Pattonsville, VA", or "Shot in Bakersville, NC", or "Shot five miles north of Gattlinburg, TN" so on and so on. Hollywood gets wind of it. Now it gets blown all out of reason. They are hiring actors to play what they think are hillbillies. There is nothing more pathetic than someone trying to play a hillbilly that don't know the language. We must remember there was only two of those people. And since they never got out to associate with anyone, to learn our customs, they are and always will be full-fledged 100% all Yankee.

Some of my friends are very interested in finding Billy Ed and Eddy Bill. So they are offering a $10,000.00 reward to anyone who can find and talk them into coming out of the mountains. Now to keep anyone from getting a New York idea, they will need to identify the family tree, which is well documented. Just one name wrong would make the offer null and void.

THE LOG CHAIN

When I was a kid there were no store bought toys, we had to improvise and we always came up with something to play with. When I was about nine years old I had the wheels turning trying to think of something new. (my older brother Henry, always said that I had my wheels spinning.)

We had this big log chain that was about twenty feet long laying in the barn and right next to it was a 60 gallon empty steel barrel. Ah ha! we have a game. This was something my sisters would play with me without strings attached. We would stand the barrel on end and see who could drag the chain across the top of the barrel without the chain falling off or the barrel turning over. The first one to drag the chain all the way across was the winner. Now you will just have to imagine he sound this made.

Well for me there was side effects I got very attached to that sound. To this day I still crave to hear it. The problem is, it is not easy to find a twenty foot log chain anymore.
When the urge comes on strong I have a good neighbor that lets me go over and start his Chrysler a few times.

MORLEY FRAMED
The true stories begin

Money was very hard to come by. Cousin Morly owed a local doctor on a bill that he couldn't pay. The doctor told him he would accept a half gallon of Albert's moonshine as payment in full.

Morly came to my dad and talked him out of a half gallon of moonshine and left to see the doctor. He ran out of gas before he got there. He took the half gallon of moonshine and hid it in a stump about three hundred feet off the road. He had to walk about a mile to get gas. When he got back to the car a deputy sheriff was waiting with a local friend.

The sheriff wanted to search the car. Morly knew the moonshine was not in the car, so he gave his okay. To Morly's surprise, the deputy found a quart of moonshine behind the back seat. The deputy arrested Morly and took him to the police station in Gate City. Morly got out on bail and came to see my dad. They went and got the whiskey from the stump and paid the doctor. Morly was hoping the Deputy would help him clear himself at the trial, but it didn't happen. Morly was sentenced to one year in prison. At this time all my relatives were very upset.

Let me stop here and explain something. When I was a kid all my relatives were very close, and I guess you could quote Louis L'Amour on the Sacketts: "If you nudge one of them, they all wake up". Also my relatives had the highest respect for a peace officer. For example we were allowed to keep a gun at the still because of the rumors of a wild panther in the country. But my dad said, "If you point a gun at the revenue officers, don't worry about what they're going to do. Worry about what I'm going to do!" Now here is a deputy that has

violated one of the laws he is sworn to uphold. If that moonshine belonged to Morly, he would have said so. This will not go unsettled!

Over the next several months the deputy had tires shot out several times and two radiators shot. One morning he was setting on the porch having a cigarette and a cup of coffee. He took a long puff on his cigarette and a sip of coffee, he set the cup on the handrail and out of the woods nearby came a bullet that busted his cup. That day he left the country not to be seen again for many years.

THE COWBOY

There is a rumor going around that some of the people from the mid to late 1800's are still around. Well I did some research on this and found it to be true. Now it does not mean that we have 150 year old people in our midst, what it means is that like minded people have stayed as close as possible to the same kind of profession. For example:

THE HORSE TRADER*
That horse owned by a little old lady that only rode it to church and back.

***USED CAR SALESMAN**
That car was owned by a little old lady that only drove it to church and back.

THE REGULATOR*
Never did an honest day's work in his life.

***THE BUREAUCRAT**
Never did an honest day's work in his life

THE RUSTLER*
What you work hard to get, most of it belongs to them.

*THE TAX ENHANCHER
What you work hard to get, most of it belongs to them.

THE HORSE THIEF*
Used to be hung on the spot.

*THE CAR JACKER
Cannot hang him on the spot.(To many lawyers.)

THE COWBOYS*
(Knights of the Range)
There is not enough room in this book to give credit the Cowboy deserves. But there is no doubt that he was a hard working, honest and ready to help in any hardship. Oh there was the occasional rouge. But justice (noose, colt) soon caught up with him.

*THE TRUCK DRIVERS
(Knights of the Highway)
Still hard working, honest, dependable and ready to help in any emergency. Most are family men that must be away from home weeks at a time.

I am told that most have a military background. And yes, occasionally there is a rouge. Like the one we recently had here in North Carolina that killed two people. Well the news media went into a frenzy. As usual they aim in the wrong direction. They want more laws for truckers. The laws were already on the books that would have put this rouge in jail, and prevented those two death's had they been enforced.
The truckers do not need more laws. What is needed is for

our justice system to be fixed and educate the car drivers.

Lets look at some numbers from the North Carolina Trucking Association. America's trucks hauled 5.5 Billion tons of freight in 1994, 55% of all freight volume. Truckers serve every community in America., 77% of communities are served exclusively by trucking and no other freight mode. Truckers travel more than 152 billion miles annually. More than 41,000 people died on Americas roads in 1995, 88% of those fatalities trucks are not involved in any way. Of the accidents causing the remaining 12% of the fatalities, where a truck was involved 72% were caused by the car driver. From 1985-1995 fatal accidents by big trucks was cut by 39% while increasing the miles driven by 41%.

Alcohol use by truck drivers on duty is almost non-existent. In a random roadside Government study only two tenths of òne percent of all truck drivers showed even the slightest measurable amount of alcohol in their systems. Only 1.3% of truck drivers involved in fatal accidents were found to be intoxicated. Compared to 19.2% for car drivers.

Mile for mile truck drivers have a accident rate less than half that of car drivers. So what it looks like is that the truck drivers are the best and safest drivers in the world. So lets all give a big thumbs up to the truckers. No the cowboy is not dead, he just traded his horse for a 18 wheeler and his rope for a C.B. (Hopefully he still has his six gun)

THE RIVER

In my mid-teens, I was spending a lot of time in Kingsport. For a while, I sold Ice Cream from a three-wheeled bicycle buggy until I outgrew it. Then I started working for McCurdy Construction in Highland. It was owned by a fine gentleman by the name of Noel McCurdy.

In the middle of January, one day, several of the employees along with three of Noel's sons, including Allen, who fancied himself somewhat of a gambler, were sitting around the office telling tall tales when the subject came up about a job we had over on the Holsten River when the weather broke. We decided to go look it over. All of us piled into two pickup trucks and Noel's big Buick Roadmaster.

We had been at the location about fifteen minutes, discussing what had to be done and how to do it.

We were ready to leave, when someone looked down at the river and made the comment that it must be real cold because of all the mushy ice running in it. I said for ten dollars, I would wade out into the river until the water was waist deep then dunk all the way under.(now here I go again letting my mouth outrun my brain).

In those days, you could do with ten dollars what it would take way over one hundred dollars to do now. Allen pulled a roll of bills out of his pocket that was big enough to choke a horse to death. He peels off a ten and hands it to me and in I went, clothes and all. That eight mile ride home in the back of a pickup was not very comfortable.

THE SALT

I remember hearing this story when I was very young. I could not remember the names. Just recently I visited some of my older relatives, and they said they remembered the story but couldn't remember the names either.

We'll call them John and Rebecca. About 9 o'clock one morning a stranger knocked on the door, and Rebecca answered. The stranger said he was hungry and would like to get something to eat. Rebecca said all right but he would have to wait until the men came in from the fields at noon for dinner. For hard working farmers in those days, the noon meal was the main one; so it was called dinner, and a heavy table was set.

About 11 o'clock the stranger went outside to get some wood for the cook stove. Rebecca started to salt the beans when their daughter told her the stranger already had salted them. When the men came in to wash up on the porch, Rebecca went out and told John what happened. John told the other men what to do. They sat down at the table, and the first thing that was passed around was the beans. Everyone put some on their plate except the stranger. He said he didn't like beans. John dished some on his plate and said he should try them. The stranger said no he wouldn't eat them. John pulled a .38 pistol out and pointed it right between his eyes and pulled the hammer back and said eat them. The stranger ate about four or five bites and fell over dead.

They never did find out where he came from or who he was, or why he "salted" the beans.

THE HANGING ROCK

This story was told to me recently by an elderly gentleman by the name of R Robbins. He knew my uncle who was born in 1870, and my uncle told him this story.

When my uncle was about ten years old, two Indians that seemed to be braves were pulling a travois with a sick old Indian in it and they stopped at his house. They were looking for a place called Hanging Rock. They needed to find it because it was a trail mark.

My uncle's father explained to them that about a mile away there used to be a big rock hanging out over the cliff, but it had fallen off and dammed up the creek. They figured that must be the place; so they left and camped on the mountain about three miles away. They were there about a month. Someone said they were digging roots and getting bark from some trees and several wild berries. When they went away, the old Indian was walking and they left the travois.

KNEE CAPPER

My grandfather sold farm implements, like mowing machines and hay rakes that ran on mule power. He had a general store and farmed the fields at home. According to my dad, Grandfather was a very handsome man.

One time there was this woman who lived about twenty-five miles away that had been writing to Grandfather until one day my grandmother got hold of a couple of the letters. This didn't set well with her. One day the woman rode up on a horse and went into the general store where Grandfather was working.

From the house nearby, my grandmother was looking through the window and saw her go in. Grandmother grabbed her pistol and went over to the store, and walked right up to the woman and shot her in the knee. Now the interesting thing about this story is, the woman was a very close relative, I believe an aunt, of a well known actor in Hollywood who once played Patton.

THE SHOOT OUT

My dad had a good friend named Martin Robbins, who lived about a mile away. There wasn't any road between their houses but a well worn path. About a year before I was born, someone started some vicious rumors about them. Nobody, including Martin, knew which family started it. In those days a lot of people carried a pistol for protection from all kinds of varmints. My dad was in Gate City one day and met Martin on the street. Martin was very angry and told my dad when they met again Dad had better go for his pistol because he was going to shoot him. My dad didn't pay much attention to what he said because he didn't think Martin would carry out his threat.

A few days later Dad went down to the fork in the road where everyone had their mailboxes. Standing by the mailboxes were Martin and a doctor setting on a horse. Dad figured he would just walk on by to his mailbox, but as he was about to pass them, Martin grabbed his pistol and started shooting. My dad was shot once in the jaw. They were so close Dad had powder burns on his face and couldn't see for a few seconds. He went for his pistol which only had three bullets in it and shot three times where he thought Martin was standing. Martin was hit once in the side of his head.

Martin's brother lived about one quarter mile away and Dad saw him run into his house and figured he was going for a rifle. Dad's pistol was empty and he had no way to get away fast enough. He asked the doctor for his horse but the doctor said, "no one is getting my horse." Dad shoved his pistol up under the doctor's arm and said, "I am taking your horse." The doctor said, "Please Mr. Brouke, just give me time to get off."

As my dad was riding away, Martin's brother started shooting at him but Dad was not hit again. Martin had to be taken to the hospital where they removed the bullet through his ear.

Later there was a trial, and my dad was sentenced to six months in jail for stealing the doctor's horse. Fortunately no one was hurt seriously. One of the reasons was my dad was using cheap bullets. Awhile after my dad got out of jail, he was passing the bottle with Martin.

THE WHITE FLAG

This is the story my dad told me several times about one of the times Harry Malcom came to visit us. He just drifted in and would stay with us for awhile, then move on to someplace else. He would usually come back whenever he was in the area. Today he would be considered retarded, but the whole family liked him and he was a hard worker.

One Sunday a bunch of my relatives were sitting on the porch, and Harry was with them. There was a big hornet's nest in the eves of my grandfather's house. It must have been twenty-five feet up to it. Cousin Rufus had just come back from fighting in Germany during World War One, and was talking about the white flag and how you never shoot at the enemy when they held it up. Harry wanted to know if it would work on the hornets? Rufus said he didn't think it would. My dad just couldn't pass this one up, so he told Harry that it would work. Harry said, "My goodness man, let's get the ladder." Harry climbed up the ladder with a big stick and punched it into the nest. My dad was standing a few steps away with the white flag. The hornets came swarming out and didn't touch Harry; but they went right for my dad and he was stung fifteen or twenty times.

Harry was mad at Dad for a long time and called him a coward for running with the white flag.

THE CHICKEN

My uncle Drake was the most stubborn, independent but honest man I ever knew. I have a cousin named Tell, who is a prankster and an agitatizer. He no doubt as me beat by a long shot.

During World War II, Tell and Drake went to Kentucky to work in the mines. This was when most things were rationed. They had been working about two weeks and living on cabbage and potatoes. After work one day they were sitting on the back porch talking about how they wished they had some meat. The neighbor closest to where they were staying had a chicken house about half way between the houses. All of a sudden they started looking at that chicken house, and Tell asked Drake if you needed ration stamps to eat chicken. Drake said he didn't think so. Tell went to get the lard. When he got back Drake had a chicken cut up ready to fry.

A few days later they went to see the neighbor and Drake explained to him how one of his chickens got in the kitchen and when they tried to chase it out, it broke its neck so they had to eat it. Drake said they came over to pay for it. The neighbor said, "I think I have lost several of my chickens that way, but you are the first ones to pay for them."

THE ANVIL

My older brothers had a friend named F. Wilson and they use to drink a lot together. F. was at our house one Saturday night and they were passing the bottle. We had a big, long porch on our house. You had to go through the door and turn left to get to the steps on the end. We had been working on the handrails at that time, and they were missing. It was about an eight foot drop if you walked straight through the door and off into the yard where we had a big anvil.

F. was feeling no pain when he left at about eleven o'clock Saturday night. At seven o'clock Sunday morning, my sisters went outside and found F. Wilson just getting up off the ground. We figured he went straight off and hit his head on the anvil. He dusted himself off and said, "Now you see what you made me do?"

THE PLOW

There are some people that don't know when you are plowing on the side of a hill you have to keep the furrows running along the hill straight. If they start running up and down, the top soil will wash off, and if this happens you have to make short passes on the low end to catch it up. To plow on a hillside you have to have a turning plow. That is when you get to the end, the plow point and mole board is turned over so you can plow going back because you can't turn the ground up hill.

My brother Henry was plowing and had just turned around at the end and started back, when he looked at the other end and there stood two revenue officers. He had a pint bottle half full of moonshine in his pocket. He realized they were watching him and he was sure they would get him. He was wearing a pair of big bulky overalls with enough room to drop a watermelon through the legs. He eased that bottle out of his pocket and dropped it though the legs into the furrow. Then he went a few more feet and turned around and covered it up. The moonshine was never found.

THE FEATHER BED

My uncle Milken bought a farm about a mile off the road. There had been a gate which had been taken down at the right of way into it, which he shared with two other families. Uncle Milken had mules and some cows so he put the gate back up. One of the neighbors came and said there had never been a gate there and he should take his down. When Milken refused to take the gate down, the neighbor sued him. Uncle Milken could talk a hungry raccoon out of a corn field; so he decided to be his own lawyer. The neighbor had a witness that swore there was never a gate there. Milken knew something about this witness. When he got up to cross examine him he said, "You tore that feather bed you stole getting through the gate didn't you?" The man said "Judge, I tore it all right, but I didn't steal it". The Judge pounded his gavel and said, "The gate stays. Case dismissed."

THE PADDLE

Since I was the family agitatizer and prankster, all done in fun, I was the one that got all the whippings. Most of them well deserved. I split my brother's pants legs with a Hawk Bill knife when I was only about five or six years old and was always getting into trouble. When I started school at nine years old, the trouble really began. I would get a whipping with a switch or sometimes with a paddle. The paddle didn't hurt as much as the switch, and that made me wonder why one hurt more than the other. One of my favorite things to do was whittling; so I decided if I made the teacher a good paddle, surely she wouldn't use it on me. I got out my knife and a good broken piece of glass for scraping, a handsaw and sandpaper, and a nice piece of red cedar and went to work. I figured if I put some small holes in it this would cut down on the air friction and make it different than the one the teacher had.

It took me several days to get it right. I used a 1/4 inch hand drill to put in several holes. The big day finally arrived, and I took it to school and gave it to the teacher. She was very pleased and held it up for all the class to see. I knew then my whipping days were over! Well you might guess...I was the first one to get whipped with it, and believe me, it worked better then the old one.

THE GAMBLE

In the early 1900's, my grandfather invested a good sum of money in three different insurance companies in New York City. Within two or three years all three had gone bankrupt. My grandfather had a little checking done and found out that all the people that had those three companies formed together into one bigger company.

They should not have stepped on a Brouke. Not all my relatives participated in the rewards of my grandfather's investment, but some did.

We had an old log barn that was built by my great-grandfather. The bottom logs were all rotten and it was about to fall down. In those days the insurance companies didn't come to see what they were insuring. My dad thought it was about time to insure the barn, and I went with him to Gate City. He wanted to make sure he picked the right company. While we were sitting in the office waiting for the man to write the policy, my dad asked him, "How is the gambling business?" The man said he didn't gamble. My dad said, "You do. You are betting that my barn won't burn, and I'm betting it will." As we were leaving the man said, "Mr. Brouke, when are you going to burn the barn?" My dad turned and replied, "The first lightning storm."

About two months later the insurance adjuster went to visit my Aunt Mattie who lived close by. When he asked her about the barn, she said, "Yes, I saw the lightning go all along the side of the barn and it burst into flames."

THE ICE CREAM SUPPER

An ice cream supper was quite an event in our part of the country. When one of the neighbors decided to have one, they would announce it by putting up signs at the crossroads and at local stores.

Usually at the fork of the road they would build a corral type stand about twelve feet square with posts in the ground and nail boards inside where the ice cream and cakes were displayed. We only had one flavor of ice cream, and that was vanilla. The ice cream was packed in dry ice to keep it cold. They put numbers on the rails around the corral and corresponding numbers in a hat. This was for a cake walk. Couples paid ten cents for the walk. The fiddle, banjo, and guitar players would play and the couples would start walking around the corral. When the music stopped the couples stopped, and a number was picked from the hat and the person closest to that number won a cake. My older brother Henry had been trying for weeks to get a date with Betty Ann. She finally said yes when he invited her to an ice cream supper that was going on near Fairview on Saturday. When the big day arrived, I was sitting on the front porch with my dad and two or three sisters. Henry was inside getting ready. He had just bought himself new pair of overall pants. They were like overalls except they had no bib, (never heard them called Jeans). He had his shoes shiny and a white shirt and tie on. When he came strutting out on the porch my dad opened his big hawk bill pocket knife and handed it to me and said "fix him." I was only five or six years old but I hooked that knife just below the belt and split those pant legs to the bottom. Henry grabbed me and started to whip me until Dad stopped him. Henry said, "Dad you have to whip him " Dad said, "No, I can't whip him. I told him to do it."

THE FISHING LESSON

When I was about ten years old I helped my brother Henry work his tobacco patch so he would take me fishing Sunday morning. Every once in a while Henry would stay out all night drinking and get home with a bad hangover.

One Sunday I got up early to go fishing, but Henry wasn't there. I waited until 11 o'clock and gave up on him and laid down for a nap. I just got to sleep when Henry dragged me out of the bed and threw me on the floor and said, "Get out of here. I need to lay down. My head is busting."

He made me really mad, and when he laid down I noticed his head was touching the wall. We had been cutting mining timber and there was a stack of it just outside the house. I got one about six or seven inches in diameter and six feet long. I held that timber like a battering ram and ran toward the house about where his head was. When I hit it the whole house shook.

Henry came tearing out of there screaming, and it was all I could do to outrun him. I guess it's a good thing I did not hit right where his head was or I might have hurt him.

THE BARREL

My brother Henry was making moonshine. He had everything ready. The mash was ready to cook and it would not wait. It had to be done as soon as possible.He hooked the mules to the sled and loaded the copper cooker and the wooden barrel on the sled and headed for the still. Mules, being what they are, decided to run away with the sled and soon there were parts of the sled and the wooden barrel all over the side of the hill. He really needed that barrel, but it was no good now.

My Aunt Suzy was married to a man named Lester who was a preacher. Henry knew Lester had a barrel so he went to see him. Lester said, "Henry you just want that barrel for making moonshine, and I will have no part in it."

That night when Lester was sleeping, Henry got the barrel. About two weeks later Lester came to see Henry and wanted a pint of moonshine for medicinal purposes so Henry gave it to him. Henry said, "Lester, I will bring your barrel back next week."

THE SHOOTOUT II

My Uncle Milken stopped by our house one day on his way home. My dad and I decided to go over to my brother's house which was on my Uncle Milken's way; so we walked along with him. Dad and I turned in at my brother's driveway as Milken continued on down the road.

There is a path running beside my brother's neighbor that comes through a hollow from another neighbor that sharpens saws. Across the road is a big hickory nut tree. We sat down on my brother's porch as Milken was getting to the neighbor's house.

There had been some more stupid lies and rumors about Milken and Martin Robbins and there was a lot of bad feelings. Martin, with a crosscut saw on his shoulder came along the path just as Milken was going by. He came up behind Milken and let that saw hit the ground.

When Milken turned around they both went for their guns. Milken was shot in the thigh as he dove for the Hickory tree. Martin was shot in the side just below his ribs and knocked into the ditch. They both emptied their guns at each other. Milken came from behind the tree and hit Martin several times with his gun. Milken walked a little more down the hill and started yelling for help. Martin was in bad shape, but he got up and went to another neighbor's and told them he was hungry.

They both ended up in the hospital on the same floor. The best thing was that neither was hurt badly. There was going to be a trial, and I was going to be a witness and get $2.00 a day. I was disappointed, because it was settled out of court and I never got my $2.00 a day.

THE STICKER

Having been born and raised in the state of Virginia ever since I can remember you had to have an inspection sticker on your car or truck. This concerns things like brakes, headlights, windshield's things that concerned the safety of someone other than the driver. I guess they figured you could take care of your own safety. My cousin Moody was a rough character and mean as they come. He had been working on an old truck with his brother Toby, and they were patching it up with anything they could find. Finally one day they got it running, and Moody told Toby they should drive it into Fairview. Toby was afraid they would be caught by the deputy but Moody assured him the deputies were all in Gate City, so off they went.

They made it to Fairview, but as soon as they pulled into the general store a deputy pulled in behind them, and they got a ticket. They could have paid a $50.00 fine, but they decided to take it to court. They drove their dad's almost new truck, the same size as their old one, into Gate City to the court house. They both swore on the witness stand that it was the one they drove when they got the ticket. The deputy took the stand and described the truck they were driving, right down to the last detail and swore to it. The judge had no choice but to turn them loose. The judge told the deputy if he found the truck of that description on their property they would have them cold. That same day the deputy took another deputy with him to find that truck. They looked high and low and after about four hours they found it. It was towed into Gate City and cousins Moody and Toby went to prison for two years for perjury.

THE WATERMELON PATCH

One of the things my dad took pride in was supervising the growing of the watermelons. I say supervising because from the time I can remember until he passed away, I never saw him actually work at anything.

Still at home at this time, I had three older sisters. There was Bonnie, the oldest, then Pearl, then Molly. I was about five years old. My brothers were much older so they were hardly ever around. When it came to play time, I was left out. My sisters would not play with me.

Once when Dad had to go away for a day on business, he made a point of putting me in charge of his watermelon patch. Now you can figure how my sisters felt.

Dad was not much more than out of sight when my sisters started treating me like a king. They wanted to play all kinds of games. This went on until about two in the afternoon. Then Bonnie suggested we go to the watermelon patch. I said no, they are not ripe yet. Well the girls kept on till they finally convinced me that it was OK. They said if Dad found out they would not tell on me.

We cut into one and it was green as all get out. We tried another, then another...all tole, we wasted about a dozen watermelons. Not one of those melons was ripe.

Dad got home about six o'clock in the evening, and you guessed it. The first place he went was the watermelon patch. When he got back to the house, he was fit to be tied. Now you have to remember that I did not go to school until I was

38

nine years old.

My Dad said, "I want to know now who was in the watermelon patch and no beating around the bush or you will all get it!"

Molly jumped up and said, "B-E-N Bonnie did it."

Out comes this long keen hickory switch, and he starts whipping the daylights out of me. All the while I'm screaming and saying, "Why are you whipping me? Molly said Bonnie did it!"

THE TOBACCO PATCH
The only true tale with flavoring added

When I was about 14 years old Brother Henry got real ambitious and decided to grow tobacco on Uncle Drake's and Uncle Milkens place along with ours. All three allotments amounted to over 3 acres. This is a lot of work considering it is done with mule power. At this time there was no chemicals to kill the weeds, worms and suckers, it had to done by hand. Now Henry asked me how much I would take to help him only when it was something he could not do by himself. So I thought it over awhile. I am thinking there is not much he will need help with. There was a suit in Kingsport I wanted to get and it cost $35.00 Now another $25.00 would be about right. I told Henry I would do it for $60.00. He agreed.
Up until Spring there is not much to do and everything was going along fine. We had built a new house and Henry got married and moved into the old house.

Then it was time for all the work to start and all of a sudden Henry says he cannot do it by himself he wants me to help with everything. It is time for a talk with Dad. He wanted to know the agreement. I told him what we agreed to and Dad says what does Henry say. I told him he says he needs help with everything. My Dad says then you are hung out to dry! From daylight 'til dark we worked. Every time Henry worked I worked with him there was no stopping for anything. With the exception of one time Henry's wife came to where we were working and said she needed some Calumet baking, powder, it was about two o'clock. Henry said if I would go to the store I would not have to work the rest of the day. Oh this is great because I can walk to Eugene's store and back in less than a hour and a half. Eugene did not have Calumet so I got Clabber Girl baking powder instead. When I got back Henry's wife had a fit, she must have Calumet!! Henry sent me to Fairview to get the baking powder, this was a 6 mile round trip. (so much for my getting into mischief time)

All through the growing season, the plowing, hoeing, pulling off the suckers and worms and topping the tobacco. We also had to build the scaffold, cutting and hanging it, pulling it off the stalk and grading it. Through all this I worked alongside Henry. Henry got through cashing all of those checks, but he did not pay me.

Now Henry had a way of pushing the button that changed me from a agitizer to a agitator. Nothing much happened the rest of the winter to speak of.

Now it is early spring and Henry is going to plant again! He says Ben if you will help me, I will pay you your sixty dollars and give you another 200 dollars when I sell the tobacco. I said "sure Henry, just as soon as Lucifer starts complaining about the cold."

One time Henry hooked the mules to the plow and pulled it to where the tobacco patch was going to be, as soon as the plow went into the ground the hame string broke on both mules and they walked out of the harness. Now Henry keeps the harness in his bedroom. Once when he was hooking up to a sled, a singletree broke right in the middle, some one had cut it almost through. He had to cut a Hickory sapling and make another. A few days later he was ready to take off with the mules pulling the sled and the doubletree broke in half.

Now he has to cut a bigger sapling. Something needs to be explained before we go on with this. I do not believe there is a more stubborn animal on Gods green earth than a mule. People call them dumb, I disagree, they know exactly what they are doing and they will run away at the drop of a hat, and you wonder where all the hats are coming from.

One thing I learned early on was you do not walk up behind and facing a mules hind feet. If one of his hind feet does not rearrange your face, that fly swatting tale will get you in the mouth, and believe me it stings!

It is a few days after the doubletree incident and I am hid in some bushes watching Henry hook up the plow. He gets hooked up and ready to go. When all of a sudden he gets that worried look on his face and starts walking around the plow and the mules looking everything over. Then he gets behind the plow and says "git up" and quickly says "whoa" and starts to checking everything out again. It is about here the mules are looking at each other and communicating. I knew what they were saying, Old Bud says to Denver "if something goes wrong this time, lets run away I know a good place to hide in the shade." Denver says to Bud "I like your idea but lets wait for another time this boy is hanging over the edge as it is." So he finally gets behind the plow and says "git up" and the beam pulls out of the plow!

It is time to set out the tobacco plants but there has been a long dry spell. Henry is hoping for rain before he sets them out. His wife is helping him this year but he would not let her help last year.

One Saturday morning they got up to find it was real cloudy, it looked like rain for sure. Most of the day they set tobacco plants out, but about 3 o'clock it cleared up with no rain.

Those plants have to be watered or they will die. But they have to wait until the sun goes down. Henry gets the mules, sled and a 60 gallon wooden barrel and went to the spring and filled it, and went to the tobacco patch, then they went home for supper. At sundown Henry and wife are ready to water the plants. But someone has bored a half inch hole at the bottom of the barrel! Henry has to catch the mules, plug the hole and fill the barrel again. It must have been fun doing all that watering by lantern light.

Another thing must be explained here. My Uncle Drake was a repairman in the coal mines and had a lot of tools to work with, he made a wagon for me that was more than twice the size of a radio flyer. It was made with white oak and the metal work was beautiful. The only thing different was the tongue, it was about three feet long with a U-bolt in the end to pull it with. But you could not fold it back and sit on the wagon and steer it. If you wanted to ride it down the hill you had to sit right on the front with your legs sticking straight out with the tongue going between your ankles to steer it.

Henry has one of his tobacco patches close to our new house and he and his wife are going to hoe it. They bring their baby to our house, get him to sleep and put him in our back bedroom. Right next to this room is this steep hill with a lot of big limestone rocks. My cousin Roland, and myself made a roadway for the wagon through and around those rocks where we come flying down on the wagon. But today we add something different. We got some old rusted tin roofing and hooked it to the back of the wagon, pulled it to the top and cut loose. That tin was a slapping off the rocks and making a lot of noise. When we got by the bedroom window we would scream as loud as we could (where we ever came up with this word I don't know)"Wobster and Calumet baking powder!! The baby would wake up and Henry's wife would have to stop hoeing and get him to sleep again. And back up the hill we would go again. After two or three times Henry took the wagon from us and locked it to my Dads trunk through the U-bolt. Then he put the key in his pocket. We took the nut off the U-bolt, pulled it off the lock and put it back on the wagon. And back up the hill we would go shouting "WOBSTER AND CALUMET BAKING POWDER!!" And so it went until the tobacco went to market.

THE COOKSTOVE

Henry had a still going for about a month, and he had a few gallons hid away. There was one more batch to be made before the still was to be torn down and hid. So he worked all night for that last six gallons. When the last jug came off, he would start mixing it for proof.

Then it was run through a copper strainer with cotton and hickory charcoal. This was always done at the still. But that morning just as he filled the last jug from the still, it started raining. So Henry brought it to the house to finish. It was about six o'clock in the morning.

Now right here I would like to explain something:

I came from a big family, my mother did almost all the work including growing the garden and the canning. She did all the washing using a galvanized tub and a wash board. As I said before, I never saw my dad work at anything, but on the other hand when my mother was awake, I never saw her when she wasn't working. I did not realize until I was much older the burdens she had to bear.

She never would have anything to do with the moon-shining, but Henry talked her into letting him finish the job in the house. Then Henry hid the whiskey and broke down the still.

At about eleven o'clock the revenuers came. There were four of them. Three of the revenuers were searching all over the outside, and one came into the house where my mother was cooking dinner on a wood burning cook stove. Henry had forgot and left the strainer on a kitchen shelf. Now there is enough whiskey left in the cotton to arrest everyone.

I was there when the revenue officer found it.

My mother's back was to him as she was working at the stove. He picked it up and smelled of it. He stood looking at my mother for almost a minute then he reached over and pulled on her apron. As she turned, he handed her the strainer.

With the strainer in her hand she continued to turn so that she faced the stove again. Without a word she lifted a cap on the stove and dumped the strainer in to the fire.

If this man is alive today, I would like to thank him.

THE MULES

One Saturday morning a whole passel of my relatives were at Cousin Hecter's house, and one neighbor from about three miles away named Biff Jaynes. Hecter was talking about how stubborn his mules were.

He said he sometimes did not get to plow a full day because the mules might decide to quit early. They would head for the barn and there was no stopping them.

Now Biff liked to talk big. He said, "No pair of mules can get the best of me. There is not a pair of mules on this Earth that I can't work."

Cousin Hector said, "Biff, you see that hillside over there? Well there is about two hour's plowing there to finish it. Let's hitch up the mules and you go plow it."

Biff said, "Consider it done."

Things went well for about a half hour when the mules started acting up and for about ten minutes they were all over the side of the hill. Then they headed for the barn.

Biff no longer had a hold of the plow. The reins were running over his shoulder and across his back and came back under his arm. Biff was almost being dragged when he started waving his arms and yelling, "Open the barn gate! I am bringing them in."

THE CORN SHUCKING

We had to grow a lot of corn. It was for feeding the chickens, milk cows, mules, and hogs. The corn was also used for moonshine and food.

In the fall of the year when the corn was gathered we would sometimes have a corn shucking. A corn shucking is just what the name says: a group of people gather to shuck corn. That's to take the outer leaves off of the ear of corn.

A lot of people would come including young men and women, sometimes a fiddle player. Most of the time it was a lot of fun. Of course, someone would always have a bottle, but no one seemed to get drunk.

Now we were having a corn shucking and Sharon was there. Henry liked her but the feeling was not mutual. One of the rules at a corn shucking was if a man found a multicolored ear, he got to kiss the girl of their choice.

Henry worked his way in close to Sharon and sat down. I guess Henry thought he was pretty smart because he kept coming up with a multicolored ear of corn. This happened five or six times before Sharon figured out it was the same ear.

Well, she broke it, along with Henry's nose.

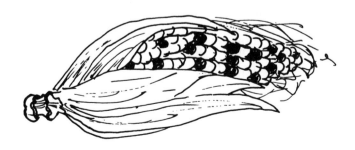

THE RACCOON

When I was very young we lived in what you would call a boxed house. It was a decent size, and it had a big attic, but the walls were only one inch thick.

At this time we had a pet raccoon. It was almost like playing with a dog. I can remember in the winter sitting around the fireplace at night with the raccoon curled up by the fire. All of a sudden it would get up and jump in someone's lap. It was mischievous as all get out.

Now my older brother, Mark, was working in Ohio. When he came for a visit he would always bring a lot of goodies that we could not get locally like oranges, grapefruit, and all kinds of nuts.

I always looked forward to his visits.

One Christmas he brought a ten pound sack of assorted hard candy along with all the other goodies. Christmas Eve it was left in the box along with all the other stuff.

When we got up Christmas morning the candy sack was empty. Every one was puzzled and looking all over for the candy, but it could not be found.

Well we found out a few days later as we were sitting by the fire and the raccoon curled up in the a corner, lazy like. All of a sudden it sat up with its eyes wide open, and then it headed to the attic. When it came back and laid down by the fire, it was chewing on a piece of candy.

We looked all over that attic but could not find one piece. For the next six months or so we would find the raccoon chewing that candy, but he never did share.

AXED

When I was in my early twenties, I left Scott County and went up North and got a job. One day at work a customer came in and threw me an apple. I was not expecting it and I didn't catch it. The man said "How come you didn't catch it?"

Any quick movement like that throws me for a second or two. The man wanted to know why. The only thing I can figure is when I was about twelve years old, I was chopping wood with a pole axe right by a wire clothesline. I was swinging it hard when the axe caught on the line and took it almost to the ground. When it sprang back the axe hit me right in the fard. He asked, "Where did the axe hit you?" I said right in the fard. He said I should show him my fard; so I pointed and told him right here. He said, "Man, that's your forehead."

He turned around and walked away laughing. I'm left standing there thinking what have I got myself into, these Yankees don't know what a fard is.

THE GROUNDHOG

On a Saturday afternoon in the 60's, I was working as a salesman up North. Just before closing there were no customers; so about seven or eight of us were sitting around a big round table telling tall tales. The Sales Manager was there and he was from Eastern Kentucky. His name should have jogged some memories from the past, but I made no connection.

I said, "Fellows, I have one that is not a tall tale. It's the truth."

When I was about twelve years old my cousin and I were coming back from the store. The road was up and down the hills and when we were in a level part of the road, kicking a Prince Albert Tobacco tin along we could see the big trees in the woods above us and scattered smaller ones below. Three revenue officers stepped out of the woods behind us and told us to wait up, they wanted to talk to us.

I knew who they were, but you have to remember I have been an agitatizer and a prankster all my life; so I told my cousin to be quiet and let me do the talking. They came up to us and I asked what the fellows were doing, groundhog hunting maybe? The older officer nodded up and down and said, "Yea, yea, we are." I asked, "How can you hit anything with those pistols? You need a rifle or shotgun." He said they were good shots and practice a lot. He asked where they could find a groundhog, maybe around where there's some water.

I know when you make moonshine you need to be around water, so I just said they might find a ground- hog anywhere. I pointed out a little tree below the road and told him there was a young one climbing up there yesterday, and I climbed up after it and stabbed it with my knife but it got away. He thought I was kidding him, but I told him no it was the truth. He sent one of his men to look, and he called back and said yes there were weeds knocked down and blood on the ground and a hole where it went in. We talked for a couple of minutes more and left for home. I stopped at my cousin's house for awhile. Later as I walked through the field on the way to my house, I merged with the officers who were coming from where we had taken down a still the day before. I ask them if they had any luck finding a groundhog. The older one said, "H___ no, but we found where one use to be."

Back around the table with the salesmen I was getting some ha ha's and no ways from the guys until the sales manager said, "Fellow's, he's telling you the truth. This is the second time I've heard that story. The first was from my uncle Charlie Redman, the revenue officer."

THE STILL

My Dad's conversation with a revenue officer.

Mr. Redman - " Mr. Brouke, we know you are making Moonshine and one day we will catch you."

Mr. Brouke - "Just what is against the law about it?"

Mr. Redman - "It is untaxed whiskey."

Mr Brouke - "If I ever wanted to make some, how do I go about paying the taxes on it."

Mr. Redman - " You can't do that!"

Mr. Brouke - "UHH HUH!"

PASSPORT

From the Ben Brouke collection, "Thoughts of a Freedom Loving Man."

I believe that everyone has to leave this earth sooner or later.

And for doing so there are two travel agents.

Everyone on this Earth is booked with one or the other.

If you are booked with the wrong one, you can change it.

I'm booked with Jesus Christ, how about you?

THE HILL TAUK DICKSHUNARY

A Glossary of
Southern Mountain
Words and Phrases

A
Above

Bove
Clem lives **bove** the sawmill.

Ackrate
That gun is very **ackrate**.
Accurate

Akern
look at that squirrel chewing on an **akern**.
Acorn

Aggervate
John can **aggervate** a man to death.
Aggravate

Aggerculture
That **aggerculture** agent is suppose to come today.
Agriculture

Alblum
That is a nice picture **alblum**.
Album

Alkihol
Put some rubbing **alkihol** on that.
Alcohol

Amblunce
Better get out of the way of that **amblunce**.
Ambulance

Amperge
The Battery in my Chevrolet has a lot of **amperge**.
Amperage

Anothern
That watermelon was good, let's go get **anothern**.
Another

Analope
Look at that **analope** over there in the trees.
Antelope

Anadote
Antidote

56

You better get some **anadote** for that snake bite.

Anafreeze   Antifreeze
There isn't any **anafreeze** in this tractor.

Anyun   Any one
That dog won't let **anyun** in.

Apperhend   Apprehend
The police are going to **apperhend** him tomorrow.

Apperhensive   Apprehensive
Wayne is **apperhensive** about doing that.

Appercot   Apricot
An **appercot** is better than a Peach.

Apern   Apron
Granny's Sunday **apern** always hung on the pantry door.

Airya   Are you
Airya going to town with me?

Argie   Argue
That boy is so mixed-up he'd **argie** with a fence post.

Ar   Arrow
He's gone hunting with a bow and **ar**.

Ax   Ask
Can I **ax** you a question?

Aspern   Aspirin
I need some **aspern** for this headache.

Asternot   Astronaut
Those **asternot's** are up there flying around somewhere.

Atall   At all

Roy and Wilber just don't get along **atall**.

Attare   Attire
His **attare** is his Sunday best.

Averge   Average
These pumkins **averge** about ten pounds.

Aukerd   Awkward
That dog is sure **aukerd**, it just triped over it's own feet.

B

Backair   Back there
Go **backair** and get that wheelbarrow.

Backerd   Backward
You have put the wagon tongue in **backerd**.

Bauld   Bald
That man is **bauld** as a bowling ball.

Bauk   Balk
That mule would **bauk** at the drop of a hat.

Baumee   Balmy
It sure is **baumee** out there today.

Banjer   Banjo
That old mountain man can make a **banjer** sing.

Baink   Bank
Gomer won't barrow any money from the **BAINK**.

Battern ram   Battering ram

58

I hit the side of the house with a **battern ram.**

Batrie   Battery
That **batrie** isn't strong enought to start the tractor.

Afore   Before
We have to fix this Dodge **afore** we go to Elmers

Beinhave   Behaving
Leonard is much nicer now that he is **beinhave.**

Bleef   Belief
It's my **bleef** that Chevrolet is a good truck.

Bleve   Believe
Do you **bleve** he'll go?

Bligernce   Belligerence
The **bligernce** of this child is terrible.

Bligernt   Beligerent
That loudmouth was very **bligernt.**

Beller   Bellow
He can **beller** louder than an old cow.

Blong   Belong
That mule does not **blong** to me.

Blow   Below
He's down **blow** the saw mill.

Bettern   Better
My truck is **bettern** his dodge.

Beverge   Beverage
Iced tea is a good **beverge.**

Biggern
Them watermelons are **biggern** they were last year.

Bigger than

Bigun
John's truck sure is a **bigun.**

Big one

Biget
I sure don't like a **biget.**

Bigot

Billard
That boy can sure shoot **billards.**

Billiard

Biller
That tent sure does **biller** out.

Billow

Bonockler
Take a look through them **bonocklers.**

Binocular

Bizair
It sure is a **bizair** storm.

Bizzare

Blackern
His truck is **blackern** an old grizzly.

Blacker than

Blackun
That cloud going over is sure a **blackun.**

Black one

Blank
That boy's ready to go at the **blank** of an eye.

Blink

Bloodiern
John cut his finger this morning and he was **bloodiern** a stuck pig.

Bloodier than

Bluern
The color of that house is **bluern** the sky.

Bluer than

Bluen

Blue one

Mary Lou got a new dress and it sure is a pretty **bluen.**

Blustern   Blustering
That boy was **blustern** around here worse than an old grizzly with a sore
paw.

Bourn   Born
Those pups were just **bourn** last week.

Borry   Borrow
Can I **borry** your hoe till I get my corn worked out?

Bothern   Bothering
Stop **bothern** the dog.

Brainiern   Brainier than
That old mule is **brainiern** a wiley raccoon.

Brainyun   Brainy one
Yep! that old mule was a **brainyun.**

Brang   Bring
Go out behind the barn and **brang** me that ax.

Brouke   Broke
Jim is so **brouke** he couldn't even buy a hamburger.

Broukun   Broke one
Yep! Jim sure is a **broukun.**

Broukern   Broker than
John is **broukern** Jim.

Brownern   Browner than
That snake is **brownern** an old rusted hoe.

Bub   Bulb
This flashlight needs a new **bub.**

Busiern   Busier than
John is **busiern** an old hen building a nest.

Buttern   Buttering
Ralph is in there **buttern** his roasting ears.

Butnen   Buttoning
Better start **butnen** your coat up.

C

Cabnet   Cabinet
Quit bothering me boy, I'm tring to build this **cabnet.**

Calsum   Calcium
Our water has a lot of **calsum** in it.

Calcalate   Calculate
I **calcalte** it's about twenty miles over there.

Caff   Calf
That sure is a pretty **caff.**

Calerbrate   Calibrate
You can **calerbrate** the brakes.

Calries   Calories
Everone is counting **calories.**

Camra   Camera
That **camra** takes a nice picture.

Caimp   Camp
Clem set-up **caimp** by that big oak tree.

Caimpen   Camping

Luther went **caimpen** with Clem.

Caimphor	Camphor

If you use **caimphor** your cold will get better.

Caimpus	Campus

Sharon is going to school and staying on **caimpus.**

Kin	Can

Kin he help me put my truck on blocks?

Canrie	Cannery

Jim is tring to get a job at the **canrie.**

Kinye	Can you

Kinye drive me to town?

Cainche	Can't you

Cainche see what your doing?

Cantileever	Cantilever

You need a big **cantileever** for that job.

Canyen	Canyon

He went to the big **canyen.**

Captal	Capital

It will take a lot of **captal** to get the business going.

Cappercorn	Capricorn

He was born under the sign of **cappercorn.**

Cappervate	Captivate

He sure knew how to **cappervate** the crowd.

Cautche	Caught you

I **cautche** stealing that watermelon

Carberhidrate	Carbohydrate

You need more **carberhidrate** in your food.

Carbernate   Carbonate
He had to **carbernate** the water.

Carbrater   Carburetor
Jim's putting a new **carbrater** on his truck.

Cardnal   Cardinal
A pretty red **cardnal** is sitting on the fence.

Carefullern   Carefuller than
He's **carefullern** a man walking a tight rope.

Cassrole   Casserole
Susie makes a good **cassrole.**

Casterate   Castrate
They had to **casterate** the bull.

Catergory   Category
You have my books in the wrong **catergory.**

Catwauk   Catwalk
They had to put a **catwauk** on the stage.

Calaflare   Cauliflower
I like **calaflare** with cheese

Cauk   Caulk
Leonard is outside trying to **cauk** the windows.

Cellerbrate   Celebrate
Lets **cellerbrate** our anniversary.

Celrie   Celery
Let's put some **celrie** in that pot.

Chauk   Chalk

Johnny go stand by the **chauk** board.

Chaimber	Chamber

The **chaimber** is off the hallway.

Chaimfer	Chamfer

He made a **chaimfer** on the edge of the table.

Chaimp	Champ

You are the **chaimp.**

Chanch	Chance

I won't take a **chanch** on that.

Cheapern	Cheaper than

These shoes are **cheapern** my last ones.

Cheapun	Cheap one

That car turned out to be a **cheapun.**

Shiverlay	Chevrolet

The thrill of owning one, just makes you shiver.

Chicrie	Chicory

The coffee has too much **chicrie** in it.

Childern	Children

The **childern** are having fun today.

Chimley	Chimney

Lets hurry up and get this **chimley** cleaned out.

Chank	Chink

Chank them little holes up.

Chitlens	Chitterlings

Lets go get some **Chitlens** and cornbread.

Quare   Choir
My sister is up there singing in the **quare.**

Circlar   Circular
Sam is putting in a **circlar** drive.

Circalate   Circulate
Let's **circalate** around and see who we can run into.

Claimp   Clamp
We need to tighten that **clamp** a bit.

Clattern   Clattering
That coon was **clattern** around all night.

Clau   Claw
The cat hurt his **clau.**

Cleernce   Clearance
There's a big **cleernce** sale on at the department store.

Clanchpourt   Clinchport
Clanchpourt is a small town in Southwestern Virginia.

Clank   Clink
The Dodge went **CLANK** when it quit.

Clost   Close
Don't follow that car to **clost.**

Clostern   Closer than
It's no **clostern** a mile.

Clostun   Close one
That game was a **clostun.**

Cloudiern   Cloudier than

The day was **cloudiern** we wanted.

Caufe   Coffee
Please don't drink all the **caufe.**

Coldern   Colder than
It's **coldern** blue blazes outside.

Coldun   Cold one
Today has been a **coldun.**

Collaberate   Collaborate
Let's get together and **collaberate** our plans.

Coult   Colt
That's a pretty brown and white **coult.**

Colyum   Column
You must read the last **colyum.**

Camaun   Come on
CAMAUN and go with me to the store.

Compnie   Company
Jim is working for a big **compnie.**

Comperhend   Comprehend
I don't think he can **comperhend** that.

Continye   Continue
Rufus will **continye** to do it till he gets it right.

Contrack   Contract
Elmer had a **contrack** to cut tobacco.

Caust   Cost
How much did that plow **caust.**

Coudje
Coudje help me hoe corn today.

Could you

Craul
The baby learned to **craul** today.

Crawl

Creamiern
The soup is **creamiern** it should be.

Creamier than

Credik
Jim can't get **credik** anywhere.

Credit

Crick
He went down to the **crick** to fish.

Creek

Crimnal
A **crimnal** broke out of jail today.

Criminal

Crankle
Billie don't **crankle** my homework.

Crinckle

Croud
This is a big **croud**.

Crowd

Crudern
He's **crudern** a hobo at a picnic.

Cruder than

Crudun
That hobo was a **cruden**.

Crude one

Cupla
Thats a nice **cupla** on our church.

Cupola

Cushiern
My chair is **cushiern** a feather bed.

Cushier than

Cushiun

Cushy one

68

Yep! My chair sure is a **cushiun.**

Cutern   Cuter than
That horse is **cutern** a speckeled pup on a red wagon.

Cuteun   Cute one
Yep! that horse is a **cuteun** allright.

Sickle   Cycle
The motor turned thru the **sickle** and quit.

D

Danderf   Dandruff
The ad said no **danderf.**

Darkern   Darker than
It's **darkern** midnight out there.

Darkun   Dark one
Man it's a **darkun** out there tonight.

Daughtern-law   Daughter-in-law
Going over to see my **daughtern-law** today.

Daun   Dawn
Clem was in the field workng before **daun.**

Deadern   Deader than
Deadern a door nail.

Deadun   Dead one
That issue is sure enough a **deadun.**

Deepern   Deeper than
My well is **deepern** the Grand Canyon.

Deepun   Deep one
The story he told was a **deepun.**

Deefault
It looks like a lot of people will **deefault** on their loan.

Default

Dellergate
I'm going to **dellergate** this job to you.

Delegate

Delivern
Luther is **delivern** the mail.

Delivering

Debidy
Daniel is a **debidy** for the county sheriff.

Deputy

Deesire
It's my **deesire** to own a Chevy.

Desire

Desprate
It is a **desprate** time we live in.

Desperate

Desternation
Nolan's **desternation** is Detroit.

Destination

Deetail
Let's get into **deetail** on this project.

Detail

Deetect
I **deetect** a little frost in the air.

Detect

Deetest
I **deetest** going to work this mourning.

Detest

Deetroit
Nolan should be in **Deetroit** about now.

Detroit

Deevelope
Let's **deevelope** a better way to do this.

Develope

Deevice

Device

70

This **deevice** is working better then before.
Didge   Did you
Didge get the message?

Jeat   Did you eat
Jeat your breakfast yet?

Differnce   Difference
There's not much **differnce** between the two of them.

Differnt   Different
This is a **differnt** truck from yesterday.

Dimmern   Dimmer than
His headlights are **dimmern** a wore out flashlight.

Dimun   Dim one
That light is sure a **dimun.**

Dare   Dire
Clem is in **dare** trouble.

Dirtiern   Dirtier than
He's **dirtiern** a hobo on a train.

Dirtiun   Dirty one
That job I did today was sure a **dirtiun.**

Disfigger   Disfigure
He tried to **disfigger** the table with his knife.

Disentergrate   Disintegrate
We put it in the ground to **disentergrate.**

Deevorce   Divorce
Do you think they will get a **deevorce?**

Daug   Dog

That is a flea-bitten **daug.**

Doen Doing
Let's get on with what we're **doen.**

Doul Dowel
This chair was put together with **doul** pins.

Doun Down
The kids went **doun** to town.

Dounair Down there
Since Eugene's store is open today, let's go **dounair** and get a sack of flour.

Draul Drawl
His speech had a very thick **draul.**

Drugs Dregs
There's some **drugs** in the bottom of that jug.

Driern Drier than
It's **driern** a hundred year old bone in the desert

Driun Dry one
That well we dug was sure a **driun.**

E

Earliern Earlier than
Mary Lou is **earliern** Sally.

Edjecate Educate
You think they can **edjecate** him at that school?

Ellervate Elevate
Ellervate my leg a little more.

Ellervation Elevation

Lets get some more **ellervation** on that gun.

Elebem   Eleven
Susie will be here at **elebem** o'clock.

Elimmernate   Eliminate
We got to **elimmernate** one more player from this game.

Embom   Embalm
That undretaker is acting strange like he wants to **embom** someone.

Emree   Emory
Grannie is filing her nails with a new **emree** board.

Empare   Empire
He thinks he's building an **empare.**

Emptiern   Emptier than
It's **emptiern** a jug at a hobo camp.

Emptiun   Empty one
That well was sure an **emptiun.**

Emalate   Emulate
He's always tried to **emalate** an actor.

Enquare   Enquire
I wish to **enquare** about a job.

Entare   Entire
I can't believe I ate the **entare** thing.

Envlope   Envelope
I'll put this in an **envlope** and mail it.

Ekal   Equal
God created all people **ekal.**

Erra   Error

I made an **erra** in judgement.

Expernce   Experience
She's got the **expernce** to do the job.

Expare   Expire
The Tags on my truck **expare** today.

Exter   Extra
I have an **exter** gun if you want to come along.

Exterdite   Extridite
The state of Georgia wants to **exterdite** him.

Exterordnary   Extraordinary
She does an **exterordnary** job.

F

Fabbercate   Fabricate
Over there is where they **fabbercate** trailers.

Factrie   Factory
Elmer got a job in the car **factrie.**

Fare   Fair
The **fare** just opened.

Faller   Fallow
His land is laying **faller**.

Famlee   Family
Jim's got a big **famlee.**

Fur   Far
It's a **fur** piece to town.

Futher   Farther

It's **futher** to work than to town.
Futhern   Farther than
My work is **futhern** Jim's.

Fastern   Faster than
That was **fastern** an old hen on a sack of corn.

Fastun   Fast one
That dragster sure was a **fastun.**

Fattern   Fatter than
That boy is **fattern** a pig ready for market.

Fatun   Fat one
That boy was sure a **fatun.**

Fathern-law   Father-in-law
I guess I have to go see my **fathern-law** today.

Fedral   Federal
We have the best **fedral** government in the world.

Feller   Fellow
Who is that **feller** coming to visit?

Fevrish   Feverish
The baby was a little **fevrish.**

Figgeration   Figuration
What kind of **figgeration** you got going here?

Figger   Figure
I **figger** we can get there about noon.

Figgerd   Figured
I **figgerd** we'd be here before now.

Figgerine   Figurine

She painted the **figgerine** beautifully.

Filtern

Filtering

He's out there **filtern** his moonshine.

Finern

Finer than

It's **finern** a ham bone in Soup beans.

Finun

Fine one

That dinner was a **finun**.

Fanger

Finger

Get your **fanger** out of that crawdad hole.

Fangerd

Fingered

A stool pidgeon **fangerd** Merle.

Far

Fire

Let's build a **far** in the fireplace.

Fard

Fired

Ralph got **fard** today.

Firmern

Firmer than

This apple is **firmern** the other one.

Firmun

Firm one

Pick through these pears and get a **firmun**.

Fishiern

Fishier than

This deal is **fishiern** the last one.

Fisheun

Fishy one

That Sam sure is a **fisheun**.

Fixter

Fixture

Jim that's a nice lamp **fixter** you have.

Flakiern

Flakier than

Your pie is **flakiern** Mary's.

Flakiun   Flaky one
That apple turnover was a **flakiun.**

Flattern   Flatter than
That tire is flattern a pancake.

Flatun   Flat one
That roof sure is a **flatun.**

Flavern   Flavoring
Put a little more **flavern** in the cake.

Flickern   Flickering
The lights must be going out, because they are **flickern.**

Flare   Flour
You put too much **flare** in the gravy.

Flare   Flower
The rose is a beautiful **flare.**

Flare   Flair
Henry always had a **flare** for the dramatic.

Flared   Flowered
The bush **flared** with Yellow buds.

Foggiern   Foggier than
Today is **fogglern** yesterday.

Foggiun   Foggy one
Tonight will be a **foggiun.**

Foke   Folk
Us hill **foke** is good people.

Foller
Foller me up the hill.

Follow

Follern
He's been **follern** me around all day.

Following

Fer
What did you do that **fer**?

For

Ferbid
I **ferbid** you to take my mule.

Forbid

Fard
I was hit in the **fard** with an axe.

Forehead

Forn
Mark bought a **forn** car.

Foreign

Fard
That gear goes **fard** instead of backward.

Forward

Formalate
We will **formalate** some good plans for this operation.

Formulate

Freekency
The **freekency** of these operations is getting closer.

Frequency

Freshern
The letuce is **freshern** the morning dew.

Fresher than

Freshun
Those watermelons look good, so pick out a **freshun**.

Fresh one

Friendliern
He's **friendliern** a half grown-pup.

Friendlier than

Friskiern
That baby is **friskiern** a room full of kittens.

Friskier than

78

Flusterate
That boy can sure **flusterate** a man.

Frustrate

Fullern
The dog is **fullern** a foundered cow.

Fuller than

Fullun
Make sure the jug is a **fullun.**

Full one

Fummergate
Jim will **fummergate** the house today.

Fumigate

Furr
That mule can plow a straight **furr.**

Furrow

Futher
Let's walk **futher** today than we did yesterday.

Further

Futhern
John went **futhern** Jim did.

Further than

Fussiern
He's **fussiern** an old mossy-horned steer

Fussier than

Fussiun
That cat's a **fussiun.**

Fussy one

Fuzziern
My sweater is **fuzziern** an old wool blanket.

Fuzzier than

Fuzziun
That peach is a **fuzziun.**

Fuzzy one

G

Galrie
Henry went to the shooting **galrie** to practice.

Gallery

Gallers   Gallows
In the old days they used to put people on the **gallers.**

Grage   Garage
Jim's building a **grage** to put his truck in.

Gathern   Gathering
Susie's out **gathern** hickory nuts.

Gauk   Gawk
Ralph always likes to **gauk** at the girls.

Genral   General
Looks like a **genral** coming this way.

Genuwine   Genuine
That's a **genuwine** Chevy.

Git   Get
Let's **git** this one.

Gitare   Get there
Tell him how to **gitare.**

Gitat   Get that
Go over and **gitat** chair.

Gitche   Get you
Go **gitche** an orange.

Gitten   Getting
Henry is **gitten** a new truck today

Gladdern   Gladder than
When Henry drove off in his new Chevrolet, he was **gladdern** a cow in
clover.

Gittnet   Getting it
He's **gittnet** in town.

Gitcher   Get your
Go **gitcher** coat and lets go

Glittern   Glittering
It was **glittern** around the Christmas tree.

Glycern   Glycerin
Better watch out for that nitro **glycern**.

Gwin   Go in
Gwin the tool box and get me that big screwdriver.

Gwinair   Go in there
I know he did it, cause I saw him **gwinair**.

Gotche   Got you
I hear you **gotche** a new Cheverolet.

Gwinside   Go inside
Gwinside and tell Martha we're ready to go.

Gwaun   Go on
Gwaun down the hill.

Gwout   Go out
Gwout and get the dog.

Gwovair   Go over there
Gwovair and tell Sam his mule is out.

Gwoutare   Go out there
Gwoutare and pick up the paper.

Gwoutside   Go outside
Gwoutside and holler for Sam.

Gwouchonder **Gwouchonder** and close the gate.	Go out yonder
Gwupair **Gwupair** on the hill and watch for Mark.	Go up there
Gwith **Gwith** Luther to the store.	Go with
Gwimmie Ask Lucy to **gwimmie** to town.	Go with me
Gwither Hand me the pail I'll **gwither**.	Go with her
Gwithem Elmer can **gwithem** to pick blackberries.	Go with him
Goen Elmer is **goen** to work tomorrow	Going
Gole Luther got a new **gole** tooth.	Gold
Guvner We're going to elect a new **guvner**.	Governor
Gradgel Let's do this job real **gradgel** like.	Gradual
Grageate That boy will never **grageate**.	Graduate
Greatun That mule John's got is a **greatun**.	Great one
Greatern That flower bed is **greatern** any I've ever seen.	Greater than

Greenun   Green one
June got a new car, and it's a **greenun.**

Greenern   Greener than
The apples are **greenern** a hornet.

Grinnich   Greenwich
The Yankees pronounce this city **Grinnich.**
(Old English)

Grimun   Grim one
Ronald wrecked his truck this morning and he's a **grimun.**

Grimmern   Grimmer than
This story was **grimmern** the last one.

Grossun   Gross one
That old hog of John's is **a grossun.**

Grossern   Grosser than
That old dog is **grossern** John's old hog.

Groun   Ground
We can plow up that new **groun.**

Groul   Growl
That old bear lays up in the woods and **grouls** all day.

Gruffiern   Gruffier than
He's **gruffiern** an old coon dog.

Gruffiun   Gruffy one
He's a **gruffiun** all right.

Garntee   Guarantee
She got a good **garntee** with her Chevy.

Guttiern   Guttier than
I do believe that man is **guttiern** George Patton.

H

Hadje   Had you
Hadje come here first you would have been okay.

Hare   Hair
We are going to get their **hare** cut tomorrow.

Haff   Half
Gomer bought a **haff** ton Chevy.

Haul   Hall
Go down the **haul,** the bedroom's on the right.

Hault   Halt
The Sheriff pointed a gun at him and told him to **hault.**

Hammern   Hammering
Elmer's building a new barn, can you hear all that **hammern?**

Handiern   Handier than
That thing is **handiern** a new Chevy pickup.

Handiun   Handy one
She is a **handiun** to have around.

Happem   Happen
I told you what would **happem** if you drove that Dodge to town.

Hapnen   Happening
What's **hapnen** at Ralph's this morning.

Hardun	Hard one
That dirt clod is a **hardun.**	
Hardern	Harder than
Them apples are **hardern** a piece of white oak.	
Harr	Harrow
Hartsel is building a new **harr.**	
Hastiern	Hastier than
He's **hastiern** a cat chasing a mouse.	
Hastiun	Hasty one
You just watch Hartsel, he's a **hastuin.**	
Haint	Haunt
There is nothing going to **haint** this house.	
Hainten	Haunting
That is a **hainten** kind of melody.	
Hauk	Hawk
Look at the **hauk** circle for a chicken.	
Heed	He would
Heed help you, but he's fixing his Dodge.	
Heaftiern	Heaftier than
My sack is **heaftiern** yours.	
Healthiern	Healthier than
He's **healthiern** a young grizzly.	
Healthiun	Healthy one
That new calf sure is a **healthuin.**	
Heaviern	Heavier than
This truck is **heaviern** the last one.	

Heaviun
I got a new gun, and it's a **heaviun**.

Heavy one

Heftiun
Try this one, it's a **heftiun**.

Hefty one

Hem
You take the **hem** and get this boat out of here.

Helm

Hep
Hep me fix my Dodge.

Help

Hern
It's not mine, it's **hern**.

Hers

Hickrie
That axe handle is made of **hickrie**.

Hickory

Hiun
Look at that hawk, it's a **hiun**.

High one

Hiern
He's flying **hiern** an Eagle.

Higher than

Har
It looks like the new factory will **har** Rufus.

Hire

Hisun
That new Chevy he's driving is **hisun**.

His one

Histrie
The **histrie** of the beginning of this country is great.

History

Holler
They went up the **holler** to pick blackberries.

Hollow

Homny
We're having **homny** grits and eggs for breakfast.

Hominy

Houp   Hoop
Watch him put the basketball through the **houp.**

Hoss   Horse
They went **hoss** back riding.
Hosswhup   Horse whip
If he was messing with the wrong bunch they'll **hosswhup** him.

Hotun   Hot one
Careful with that stove, it's a **hotun.**

Hotern   Hotter than
That Dodge is running **hotern** a three dollar pistol.

Air   Hour
It will take about one **air** to start your Dodge.

Hau   How
Hau do you think he'll do?

Haud   How did
Haud he find the place?

Haudje   How did you
Haudje get here so fast?

Haudy   Howdy
Haudy, Billy Joe Jim Bob.

Houl   Howl
Listen to my dog **houl.**

Hugeun   Huge one
Hartsel got a new truck, and its a **hugeun.**

Humrus   Humorous
Tell us about the most **humrus** man in the country.

Hidergen	Hydrogen

That **hidergen** bomb is powerful.

Hiperdermic	Hypodermic

The doctor shot him with a big **hiperdermic** needle.

Hipercondrac	Hypochondriac

There is a **hipercondrac** in my family.

Hippercrit	Hypocrite

The only **hippercrit** in my church is me.

I

Aise	Ice

Do you want some **aise** in your water?

Ideho	Idaho

Elmer went deer hunting in **Ideho.**

Idee	Idea

That was a good **idee** you had.

Idyet	Idiot

That was a **idyet** thing to do.

Ignernt	Ignorant

I saw a man do an **ignernt** thing today.

Emertate	Imitate

John tries to **emertate** Rufus.

Impervise	Improvise

If you don't get it done one way, **impervise** and do it another.

Inair	In there

It's **inair,** please bring it out.

Incorperate His company is fixing to **incorperate.**	Incorporate
Incrimmernate The police are going to **incrimmernate** him.	Incriminate
Infrekent This is getting to **infrekent.**	Infrequent
Ank I need some **ank** in my pen.	Ink
Anklen Mom and Dad don't have an **anklen** about the party.	Inkling
Innervate Lets **innervate** another way.	Innovate
Inquare Lets go and **inquare** about Bob.	Inquire
Inspare Reading a good book will always **inspare** me.	Inspire
Instaul He's ready to **instaul** a new motor in his Dodge again.	Install
Instergate Melvin will **instergate** trouble.	Instigate
Instertute Let's see what is happening a the Bible **instertute.**	Institute
Insterment Did you see the **insterment** panel on Robert's sawmill?	Instrument
Inshore We want to **inshore** the barn.	Insure

Innerst   Interest
If you put money in the bank, you will get **innerst.**

Innerfere   Interfere
Milford will **innerfere** with us.

Innermix   Intermix
We can all go in there and **innermix** like we are part of the crowd.

Innerup   Interupt
You just watch Milford **innerup** the whole thing.

Innervene   Intervene
If Peanut comes he will **innervene.**

Innerview   Interview
Our senator will give an **innerview** to that big newsman.

Intranch   Intrench
Rufus told me how the soldiers would **intranch** before a battle.

Innerduce   Introduce
Let me **innerduce** my uncle Drake.

Invove   Involve
This will **invove** a lot of people.

Innard   Inward
That porch post is leaning **innard.**

Arsh   Irish
Today we planted **arsh** potatoes.

Arn   Iron
I need to **arn** some clothes.

Izzer   Is there
Izzer any reason you can't help?

Hit   It
Hit ain't time to go yet.

Itsa   It is a
Itsa far piece to town.

Ivree   Ivory
Ralph has a knife with a **ivree** handle.

J

Jaywauk   Jaywalk
Don't **jaywauk** when you are in town.

K

Keenun   Keen one
That Chevy is a **keenun.**

Keenern   Keener than
That's **keenern** anything I've seen.

Kinnel   Kindle
Let's **kinnel** a fire in the cook stove.

Kang   King
Wilbur thinks he should be a **kang.**

Kangsport   Kingsport
Kangsport is a city in east Tennessee.

Nowd   Knew
I **nowd** he wouldn't do it.

L

Laimp   Lamp
She's reading by a **laimp** light.

91

Lanern
She lit the **lanern** and left.

Lantern

Latun
Seem's like he's always a **latun**.

Late one

Leanun
That steak was a **leanun**.

Lean one

Leanern
That boy's **leanern** an old stove up dog.

Leaner than

Leftare
He got all excited and **leftare** in a hurry.

Left there

Laig
Gomer's old mule kicked him in the **laig**.

Leg

Lepersy
I hear tell people in the old days sometimes had **lepersy**.

Leprosy

Lessen
A sack of meal cost **lessen** a sack of flour.

Less than

Letche
Ronald will **letche** borrow his mule.

Let you

Levelun
That barn site is a **levelun**.

Level one

Leever
To pry this out we need a **leever**.

Lever

Leverge
Now we have more **leverge**.

Leverage

Libul
You don't know what he's **libul** to do.

Liable

Lietun
That sack is a **lietun.**

Light one

Lietern
It's **lietern** a feather.

Lighter than

Limberun
That cucumber is a **limberun.**

Limber one

Langer
All he does is **langer** there all day.

Linger

Lank
There is a **lank** missing in his chain.

Link

Likadate
Theres a time to **likadate** and theres a time to go full tilt.

Liquidate

Livrie
Put your horse in the **livrie** and come on in.

Livery

Loug
Today Bob cut the biggest **loug** I ever saw in my life.

Log

Loosun
That motor is not tight in there. It's a **loosun** .

Loose one

Loosern
It's **loosern** a cannon in the German army.

Looser than

Loudun
That young man is a **loudun.**

Loud one

Loudern
He's **loudern** an old grizzly with a sore paw.

Louder than

Lousiern
It's **lousiern** a bad haircut.

Lousier than

Lousiun Lousy one
That truck is a **lousiun**.

Lowun Low one
A snake is a **lowun**.

Lowern Lower.than
It's **lowern** a snake in a wagon track.

Lubbercate Lubricate
He's going to **lubbercate** his truck.

Luckiern Luckier than
Ted is **luckiern** a bear in a honey tree.

Luckiun Lucky one
He sure is a **luckiun**.

Lumpiern Lumpier than
It's **lumpiern** grandpa's mashed potatoes.

Lumpiun Lumpy one
That basket ball has been kicked around too much, and it's a **lumpiun**.

Madun Mad one
Rufus can't start his Dodge again. He' a **madun**.

Maddern Madder than
He's **maddern** a wet hen.

Maul Mall
I was born long before there was a shopping **maul**.

Mault Malt
You have to have good **mault** to make moonshine.

94

Manafacter   Manufacture
The new factory will **manafacter** widgets.

Marvel   Marble
If you want to win a lot, you have to have a good **marvel** to shoot with.
Marr   Marrow
There is a lot of **marr** in this bone.

Marshmeller   Marshmallow
We roasted **marshmellers** at the pinic.

Mavrick   Maverick
He's still driving that old **mavrick.**

Medder   Meadow
Go out in the **medder** and pick some flowers.

Meanun   Mean one
That old Grizzly is a **meanun.**

Meedyum   Medium
This should be about **meedyum** size.

Meekern   Meeker than
That horse is **meekern** a kitten.

Meller   Mellow
Those apples are soft and **meller.**

Memree   Memory
My **memree** is not what it used to be.

Mercree   Mercury
Claude traded his **Mercree** for a Chevy.

Messiern   Messier than
That boy is **messiern** an old hog.

95

Messiun
Watch out for Rufus, because he's a **messiun**.

Messy one

Mightiern
Luther thinks he's **mightiern** Superman.

Mightier than

Mightiun
The Lord God is a **mightiun**.

Mighty one

Mildun
The horse we have is a **mildun**.

Mild one

Mile
It's twenty **mile** to town.

Miles

Minral
There is a lot of **minral** in this water.

Mineral

Minner
Let's bait our hooks with a **minner**.

Minnow

Misfar
His gun will **misfar** every so often.

Misfire

Mixter
We got the right **mixter** in this motor.

Mixture

Modrat
I'm getting along **modrat** well.

Moderate

Moldiern
It's moldiern a spoiled loaf of bread.

Moldier than

Moldiun
This pie is spoiled It's a **moldiun**.

Moldy one

Moodiern
He's **moodiern** an old hungry possum.

Moodier than

Moodiun — Moody one
I never saw such a **moodiun.**

Mo — More
Why did you plant **mo** corn?
Morn — More than
My sister got **morn** me.

Mussketer — Mosquito
I believe thats the biggest **mussketer** I ever saw.

Muthern-law — Mother-in-law
My **muthern-law** is coming for a visit.

Motorsickle — Motorcycle
Roy was riding around on his **motorsickle** awhile ago.

Muddiern — Muddier than
This creek is **muddiern** the Mississippi River.

Muddiun — Muddy one
Don't fish in that pond. It's a **muddiun.**

Muffer — Muffler
He's over there putting a **muffer** on his truck.

Muggiern — Muggier than
Its **muggiern** July in the swamp.

Muggiun — Muggy one
Today is a **muggiun.**

Mushmelon — Muskmelon
I have seen Ronald sneak into the **mushmelon** patch.

Muttern — Muttering
Qnit **muttern** around and speak up.

Mutchel
They both are staying **mutchel.**

Mutual

Mistree
It's a **mistree** what's happening.

Mystery

N

Necked
He's **necked** as a Jay bird.

Naked

Narr
The road through the hollow is **narr.**

Narrow

Nastiern
That cook is **nastiern** I've ever seen.

Nastier than

Nacherly
It's one of those things yo do **nacherly.**

Naturally

Nearern
Eugene's store is **nearern** Orries.

Nearer than

Neatun
Mary Lou is a **neatun.**

Neat one

Neatern
That Chevy is **neatern** anything I've seen.

Neater than

Nerviern
She's **nerviern** a coon in a bee tree.

Nervier than

Nerviun
Roy rode that bucking mule to the store He's a **nerviun.**

Nervy one

Newun
Milken got a Chevrolet It's a **newun.**

New one

98

Newern
My truck is **newern** yours.

Newer than

Nextun
The **nextun** is mine isn't it?

Next one

Nippiern
It's **nippiern** frost in the morning.

Nippier than

Nippiun
Today has been a **nippiun**.

Nippy one

Noisiern
It's **noisiern** a fox in a hen house.

Noisier than

Noisiun
That old truck is a **noisiun**.

Noisy one

Nauth
Hubert went up **nauth** to Detroit to work.

North

Nautherd
Look **nautherd** and you can see a big star.

Northward

Nuttiern
That old mule is **nuttiern** a fruitcake.

Nuttier than

Nuttiun
That cat is a **nuttiun**.

Nutty one

O

Oddun
That politician is an **oddun**.

Odd one

Oddern
He's **oddern** a three legged cat.

Odder than

Aufer   Offer
Rufus got an **aufer** on his Dodge and he took it.

Offen   Often
This is happening too **offen** for me.

Aul   Oil
He's going to change the **aul** in his truck.

Ole   Old
That plow Hugh has is a **ole** one.

Aun   On
Don't bet **aun** a crippled horse.

Onest   Once
Onest I saw two eagles fighting.

Onard   Onward
Always upward and **onard** bound.

Opree   Opera
We are going to the Grand Old **opree**.

Arnge   Orange
Now thats a big **Arnge**

Okister   Orchestra
I don't like an **okister**.

Ordern   Ordering
He's always **ordern** someone else around.

Ort   Ought
You **ort** to get a Chevy.

Air   Our
We are going to plant **air** corn tomorrow.

Airn   Ours
You can't have that horse, its **airn**.

Airsef   Ourself
We'll do this job **airsef** .

Outare   Out there
It's **outare** behind the barn.

Outerd   Outward
Point it **outerd** and be carefiil.

Overn over   Over and over
Jim tells that same story **overn over**.

Ovair   Over there
Look **ovair** on that hill, can you see that big ground hog?

P

Pare   Pair
I got a new **pare** of shoes today.

Paleun   Pale one
He's kind of sickly and a **paleun**.

Palern   Paler than
He's **palern** that old horse of John's.

Paam   Palm
If you're trying to catch a bird, be careful of what you get in your **paam**.

Painter   Panther
There's a wild **painter** around.

Pappern   Papering
She's in there **pappern** the walls.

Pareboil Parboil
Pareboil the ground hog before you fry it.

Pertickler Particular
Drake is the most **pertickler** man I ever saw.
Pardner Partner
This here is my **pardner**.

Pare Pear
I got a **pare** off that tree over there.

Perkiern Perkier than
She's **perkiern** a kitten with a ball of twine.

Perkiun Perky one
That Becky, is a **perkiun**.

Persnal Personal
Don't tell me that, it's **persnal**.

Peana Piano
Now that was some good **peana** playing.

Pickral Pickerel
Drake went out and caught a mess of **pickral** today.

Piller Pillow
My **piller** is too hard.

Pank Pink
They painted their house **pank**.

Pineer Pioneer
He was the old **pineer** breed.

Plainun Plain one
That truck is a **plainun**.

Plainern   Plainer than
It's **plainern** the nose on your face.

Plaint   Plant
We are going to **plaint** corn today.
Pouke   Poke
Bring home a **pouke** of flour.

Pouker   Poker
Get the **pouker** and stir up the fire.

Pondruss   Ponderous
That is a **pondruss** old sawmill.

Poorun   Poor one
Arnold needs help. He's a **poorun.**

Plece   Police
The **plece** are fixing to pull you over.

Poorern   Poorer than
He's **poorern** a hobo.

Popler   Popular
Rufus was the most **popler** one at the dance.

Pourch   Porch
It's nice to sit on the **pourch** in the evening.

Postive   Positive
I'm **postive** it will work.

Poust   Post
The best fence **poust** is made of locust.

Tater   Potato
Please pass me a **tater.**

Pare   Power
That Chevy has a lot of **pare.**

Percise   Precise
Get the **percise** measurements and it will work.
Perdict   Predict
I **perdict** it will be a cold winter. .

Perfer   Prefer
Of all the trucks made I **perfer** a Chevy.

Premyun   Premium
Ham cured the right way is **premyum.**

Perpare   Prepare
I will help you **perpare** those greens.

Perservative   Preservative
Don't eat that. It has too much **perservative** in it.

Perserve   Preserve
Watch him **perserve** all the fruit.

Persume   Presume
I **persume** you are going with me.

Pertend   Pretend
Don't **pertend** you don't know, when you do.

Purtiern   Prettier than
She's **purtiern** a speckled pup on a red wagon.

Purty   Pretty
That new girl at the store sure is **purty.**

Pervent   Prevent
We should **pervent** him from going.

Perceed   Proceed
Perceed with what you were doing.

Perfess   Profess
She will **perfess** she loves him.
Permote   Promote
Let's **permote** Jim to that job.

Pernounce   Pronounce
There is a lot of words Jim can't **pernounce.**

Pertect   Protect
A sheriff is elected to **pertect** the citzens.

Pertest   Protest
I will **pertest** this move.

Pervide   Provide
If you will work for us we'll **pervide** you with tools.

Pervoke   Provoke
Don't **pervoke** Rufus today.

Prize   Pry
Get a big stick and **prize** this wheel off.

Puffiern   Puffier than
He's **puffiern** an old stuffed posssum.

Puffiun   Puffy one
That dog has been eating all day, and he's a **puffiun.**

Pup   Pulp
Henry is up there on the hill cutting a load of **pup** wood.

Pureun   Pure one
That pint of Moonshine is a **pureun.**

105

Purern
That piece of silver is **purern** the driven snow.

Purer than

Purpelun
Sally got a new car and it's a **purpleun.**

Purple one

Q
Quick one

Quickun
Did you see that rabbit go? He was a **quickun.**

Quickern
He's **quickern** a mule out of a briar patch.

Quicker than

Quietun
That kid Billy is a **quietun.**

Quiet one

Quietern
It's **quietern** a church mouse on Sunday.

Quieter than

R
Radish

Reddish
Pass me a **reddish** please.

Druther
This is hard work. I'd **druther** be fishing.

Rather

Recknen
My **recknen** is all out of whack.

Reckoning

Reecover
We will **reecover** our tool's that were stolen.

Recover

Redun
Rosemarie got a new dress. It's a **redun.**

Red one

Redern
This truck is **redern** a cardinal.

Redder than

Refernce   Reference
I have a good **refernce.**

Ragler   Regular
It's just a **ragler** still, nothing fancy.

Ragalate   Regulate
It seems like our government is going to **raglate** everything.

Reeject   Reject
If you **reeject** this one there won't be another.

Reejoin   Rejoin
Yes, you should **reejoin** the Army .

Reelible   Reliable
When it comes to his job, Cletus is **reelible.**

Reepare   Repair
Go help Marvin **reepare** his Dodge.

Reepent   Repent
Bob has been a bad boy. He had better **reepent.**

Repersent   Represent
Milken is going to **repersent** himself.

Repermand   Reprimand
Rufus was late for work and he got a **repermand.**

Reepublic   Republic
This is supposed to be a **reepublic.**

Requare   Require
I **requare** an honest day's work for an honest day's pay.

Reespect	Respect

A little **reespect** will help.

Reestore	Restore

Alfred thinks he can **reestore** his Model A.

Retar	Retire

Salley will **retar** in three years.

Retard	Retired

Rufus has so much free time you would think he was **retard.**

Reetread	Retread

A **reetread** will be all right for the Dodge.

Reeverse	Reverse

I got my fluid drive DeSoto on top of a hill and couldn't get it into **reeverse.**

Reevover	Revolver

Milkin and Martin shot each other with a **reevover.**

Reeward	Reward

There was a big **reeward** on John Dillinger.

Rewarr	Rewire

He's going to **rewarr** his Dodge.

Richun	Rich one

I saw a man in town driving a Cadillac, he's a **richun.**

Richern	Richer than

That feller is **richern** a king.

Ritare	Right there

Let's build a chicken house **ritare** next to that tree.

Ranch	Rinse

Johnny go **ranch** the soap off your face.

Riskiern   Riskier than
This is **riskiern** betting on a lame horse.

Riskiun   Risky one
This location is a **riskiun.**

Robrie   Robbery
Peanut arrested him for **robrie.**

Rockiern   Rockier than
This field is **rockiern** a stone quarry.

Rockiun   Rocky one
That big hill called Possum dome is a **rockiun.**

Rouf   Roof
I believe that everyone in their life should own one
building with a flat **rouf** and one Chrysler product.

Roum   Room
Go in the back **roum** and wake up Henry.

Roumiern   Roomier than
This house is **roumiern** the other one.

Roomiun   Roomy one
That new Cadillac is a **roomiun.**

Ruffun   Rough one
Marvin is sure a **ruffun.**

Ruffern   Rougher than
He's **ruffern** a cob and twice as corney.

Rudern   Ruder than
He's **rudern** a hobo at a Fourth of July picnic.

Rudun   Rude one
The man who barked at the waitress sure is a **rudun.**

Rernt   Ruined
That new Plymouth Rufus bought a year ago **rernt** already.

S

Sadun   Sad one
When Billy's Dodge broke down again. He was a **sadun.**

Saddern   Sadder than
He was **saddern** Jeff was when he drove his truck into the creek.

Saltiern   Saltier than
He's so mean, he's **saltiern** an old alligator.

Saltiun   Salty one
If you put too much salt on your tomato it will be a **saltiun.**

Saave   Salve
Better put some **saave** on that bee sting.

Sanwich   Sandwich
Two hot dogs split in half and fried makes a good **sanwich.**

Scap   Scalp
Henry was chopping wood and a chip flew up and cut his **scap.**

Scair   Scour
Better boil some water and **scair** that pot out good.

Seed   Seen
I **seed** John riding his mule to the store.

110

Seff   Self
The new service station is **seff** service.

Seprate   Separate
We need to **seprate** the Apples from the Pears.
Serus   Serious
Albert is **serus** about joining the army.

Sebem   Seven
There are **sebem** days in a week.

Shadder   Shadow
That ground hog has seen his **shadder.**

Shaddery   Shadowy
Those pictures we took are very **shaddery.**

Shaller   Shallow
The Creek is real **shaller** lately.

Sharpun   Sharp one
That Hawk bill knife he carries is a **sharpun.**

Sharpern   Sharper than
His knife is **sharpern** a razor.

Sheff   Shelf
On the kitchen **sheff** is a pint mason jar, please. go get it.

Sherf   Sheriff
Peanut will some day be elected **sherf.**

Shiftiern   Shiftier than
Better watch him 'cause he's **shiftiern** a weasel in a hen house.

Shiftiun   Shifty one
He's a **shiftiun** all right.

Shangle   Shingle
Come on up and help me **shangle** my roof.

Shortun   Short one
Looks like you go first. I got the **shortun.**
Shortern   Shorter than
Your car is **shortern** mine.

Share   Shower
John is putting a **share** in his house.

Sickun   Sick one
Henry drank some bad moonshine, and he's a **sickun.**

Sickern   Sicker than
He's **sickern** a weak cat in a dog fight.

Simlar   Similar
This watermelon is **simlar** to the last one.

Simalate   Simulate
Ralph is going around with a big flashlight trying to **simalate** a freight train.

Sangle   Single
Yes, Jane is still **sangle.**

Sangler   Singular
It's the **sangler** most important thing you can do right now.

Sank   Sink
Martha has a newfangled kitchen **sank.**

Sistern-law   Sister-in-law
This is my **sistern-law** from Florida.

Sitare   Sit there
Don't just **sitare** like a bump on a log.

Slickern   Slicker than
That boy is **slickern** a con man in a poker game.

Slickun   Slick one
Ronald dropped varnish on his foot and he was a **slickun.**

Slimun   Slim one
That rail you put on the fence is a **slimun.**

Slimern   Slimmer than
Rufus is **slimern** a bean pole.

Slang   Sling
Rufus just killed a pheasant with a **slang** shot.

Slowun   Slow one
It's like watching a turtle 'cause he's a **slowun.**

Slowern   Slower than
That mule is **slowern** molasses in January.

Smallun   Small one
You get the **smallun** and I'll get the big one.

Smallern   Smaller than
Your barn is **smallern** mine.

Smartun   Smart one
The old red mule is a **smartun.**

Smoothern   Smoother than
Elmer is **smoothern** a fox after a rooster.

Snappiern   Snappier than
He's **snappiern** a soldier in a parade.

Snappiun   Snappy one
Boy, that red convertible is a **snappiun.**

Softun   Soft one
That feather bed sure is a **softun.**
Softern   Softer than
It's **softern** a Teddy Bear.

Soljer   Soldier
Come to think of it; Rufus does look like a **soljer.**

Sove   Solve
Let's **sove** this problem and get going.

Summers   Somewhere
Peanut took a trip up North **summers.**

Sauth   South
I just love living in the **sauth.**

Spelt   Spelled
In the test today, Leonard **spelt** one word wrong.

Spiciern   Spicier than
It's **spiciern** chili pepper.

Spiciun   Spicy one
That hot dog was a **spiciun.**

Sprang   Spring
We keep our milk down at the **sprang** to keep it cool.

Stares   Stairs
Climb the **stares** and go to bed.

Stauk   Stalk
That's the tallest corn **stauk** I ever saw.

114

Staul   Stall
The old red mule is trying to kick out of his **staul.**

Stiffun   Stiff one
It's a **stiffun** because it has too much starch.
Stiffern   Stiffer than
He stands **stiffern** a fence post.

Stipalate   Stipulate
We have to **stipalate** it in writing.

Stirp   Stirrup
Henry got his foot caught in the **stirp** and had trouble getting off the
mule.

Storge   Storage
John already had his corn in **storge.**

Straitun   Straight one
The road between here and Gomer's is a **straitun.**

Strang   String
Tie a **strang** around it.

Stuffiern   Stuffier than
It's **stuffiern** a mine tunnel in here.

Stuffiun   Stuffy one
The way he struts around he acts like a **stuffiun.**

Suffern   Suffering
The milk cow got caught in a briar patch and she is **suffern.**

Shore   Sure
Shore enough she is coming up the hill now.

Swaller   Swallow
I don't believe he can **swaller** the whole thing.

Swang   Swing
We got a **swang** on our front porch.

T

Tackiern   Tackier than
Bill dresses **tackiern** a hobo.

Tackiun   Tacky one
That old suit is a **tackiun.**

Tauk   Talk
Let's not sit here and **tauk** all day.

Termnal   Terminal
The bus **termnal** in Gate City is not very big.

Attare   That there
Attare is a good truck.

Atsa   That's a
Atsa big watermelon you got.

Thern   Theirs
The mule you saw at John and Lucy's is **thern.**

Em   Them
When we get **em** potatoes hoed we can go to town.

Themmer   Them are
Themmer some good beans.

Air   There
Air isn't enough left to go around.

Thickern   Thicker than
Blood is **thickern** water.

Thinun   Thin one
That sandwich is a **thinun.**

Thang   Thing
Get that **thang** out of here.

Thank   Think
I don't **thank** he can do it.

Thinnern   Thinner than
Mary's jars of molasses are **thinnern** water.

Iss   This
Take **iss** hammer back to Milken.

Issun   This one
Take **issun** and go on home.

Tar   Tire
Help me put a **tar** on my car.

Tard   Tired
I am too **tard** to go to Amy's.

Backer   Tobacco
We grow about three acres of **backer.**

Tole   Told
Luther **tole** me he is going to get married.

Taleda   Toledo
Taleda is a city in northwest Ohio.

Tamarr   Tomorrow
Let's go see Rufus **tamarr.**

Tarpeda   Torpedo
The German's started using the **tarpeda.**

Tord   Toward
On the way **tord** town, stop and see Henry.
Tare   Tower
Radio station WKIN has a big **tare.**

Trueun   True one
Mary Lou sure is a **tureun.**

Truern   Truer than
Elmo is **truern** a good judge.

Chuesday   Tuesday
Chuesday is the next day after Monday.

Tweve   Twelve
Tweve donuts make a dozen.

U

Umpare   Umpire
The third base **umpare** called him out.

Unner   Under
He is hiding **unner** the bridge.

Upair   Up there
She has gone **upair** on the hill.

Upperd   Upward
Watch how fast that hawk goes **upperd.**

V

Vagernt   Vagrant
There was a **vagernt** by here yesterday.

Vampare   Vampire
There is no such thing as a **vampare.**

Vetern   Veteran
Rufus is a **vetern** of World War I.

Vugar   Vulgar
That man talks too **vugar** for me.

W

Wauk   Walk
Let's **wauk** down to Eugene's store.

Waul   Wall
That **waul** is only one inch thick.

Waller   Wallow
The hog will lay there and **waller** all day.

Warmun   Warm one
The front room is a **warmun.**

Warmern   Warmer than
Your house is **warmern** mine.

Warnt   Warrant
The sheriff has a **warnt** for Milford.

Wuz   Was
John **wuz** in town today.

Warsh   Wash
Let's go **warsh** the car.

Weakun   Weak one
Henry has been sick for three days, and he's a **weakun.**

Weakern   Weaker than
That dog is **weakern** a sick cat.

Wetun
The old mule came out of the creek a **wetun**.
Wettern
The bottom land is **wettern** I've ever seen.

Whad
Whad she get for her birthday.

Whadje
Whadje go there for?

Wheelbar
Go out behind the barn and get the **wheelbar**.

Whend
Whend Drake go home?

Whendje
Whendje get that new Chevy?

Whenev
Whenev I told you wrong?

Whenevye
Whenevye seen Ralph?

Wherd
Wherd Ralph go?

Wherv
Wherv I seen you before?

Whervye
Whervye been all day?

Whichun
Whichun do you want?

Wet one

Wetter than

What did

What did you

Wheelbarrow

When did

When did you

When have

When have you

Where did

Where have

Where have you

Which one

Whup   Whip
Watch out for Elmer, he's going to **whup** you.
Whitun   White one
It's a **whitun** with all that snow.

Whitern   Whiter than
Billy was so scared he was **whitern** a sheep.

Whuther   Whether
I don't care **whuther** you go or not.

Whoed   Who did
Whoed Ralph go to work with?

Whoedje   Who did you
Whoedje see in town?

Wholeun   Whole one
I could not eat but half and Billy ate a **wholeun.**

Whyd   Why did
Whyd Henry leave so fast?

Whydje   Why did you
Whydje take so long to plow that field?

Whyv   Why have
Whyv I not seen you for so long?

Whyvye   Why have you
Whyvye come in so late?

Widun   Wide one
I'd much rather have a **widun.**

Widern   Wider than
That car coming there is **widern** a Mack truck.

Widder   Widow
Dad has gone to take some beans to the **widder.**
Wildun   Wild one
That bear that went through here was a **wildun.**

Wildern   Wilder than
That cat is **wildern** a bear in the woods.

Willer   Willow
Who chopped down the **willer** tree?

Winder   Window
Open the **winder** a little, it's hot in here.

Wang   Wing
Look at the **wang** span on that Eagle.

Wank   Wink
I saw Elmer **wank** at Lucy.

Warr   Wire
Help me put some **warr** on these fence posts.

Wither   With her
Did you go **wither** to the store?

Wimmie   With me
Marie went **wimmie** to the store.

Woff   Wolf
There is a **woff** after the chicken.

Worsern   Worser than
The storm is **worsern** I thought.

122

X-Y-Z

Ear   Year
There are 365 days in a **ear.**

Yaller   Yellow
Jim painted his house **yaller.**

Yaul   You all
Yaul come with us if you can.

Yungun   Young one
Go get the **yungun** off the swing.

Yorn   Yours
It's not mine, it's **yorn.**

THE ROCK PEOPLE
Time for a little Freedom Tauk.   (From the Ben Brouke Collection)

A little over two hundred years ago, in order to form one of the greatest Nations the world has ever known, the American people were rounding up, shooting, hanging, putting in prison and chasing out of the country, people known as traitors and taxationists. Some of them got away and crawled under a rock. For over 100 years our country, at every level, was run by Public Servants who understood they had no power whatsoever, except what was delegated to them by the people.

But, lo and behold, the Rock People's grand and great-grand children crawled from under the rock and started to infiltrate our government and they have replaced about 8 out of 10 of our Public Servants. Today they are known as owned politicians, bureaucrats and tax enhanchers.

THE DIFFERENCE BETWEEN:
From the Ben Brouke Collection

Owned politician
Bureaucrat
Tax enhancer
Jesse James *   **

* Did it with a gun.
** Did not rob his mother.